A PLACE FOR

BUTTERFLIES

For Colin, Claire, and Caroline

—M. S.

For my new grandchild,
Andrew Jordan Bond:

welcome to the world!

—H. B.

Published by
PEACHTREE PUBLISHERS
1700 Chattahoochee Avenue
Atlanta, Georgia 30318-2112
www.peachtree-online.com

Text © 2006, 2014 by Melissa Stewart
Illustrations © 2006 by Higgins Bond

First trade paperback edition published in 2011

Book design by Loraine M. Joyner
Illustrations created in acrylic on cold press illustration board.

Printed in June 2017 by Imago in Singapore
10 9 8 7 6 5 4 3 2 1 (hardcover)
10 9 8 7 6 5 4 3 (paperback)
Revised edition

Library of Congress Cataloging-in-Publication Data

Stewart, Melissa.
  A place for butterflies / written by Melissa Stewart ; illustrated by Higgins Bond.
      p. cm.
  978-1-56145-789-2 (hardcover)
  978-1-56145-784-7 (paperback)
  1. Butterflies—Ecology—Juvenile literature. 2. Butterflies—Effect of human beings on—Juvenile literature. I. Bond, Higgins, ill. II. Title.
    QL544.2.S746 2006
    595.78'917--dc22
                            2005020495

A PLACE FOR

BUTTERFLIES

Written by
Melissa Stewart

Illustrated by
Higgins Bond

PEACHTREE
ATLANTA

Butterflies fill our world with beauty and grace. But sometimes people do things that make it hard for them to live and grow.

If we work together to help these special insects, there will always be a place for butterflies.

A Butterfly's Life

As butterflies grow, they go though four life stages. A female butterfly lays her eggs on plants. When an egg hatches, a caterpillar wriggles out. After a few weeks of nonstop eating, the caterpillar becomes a pupa. It is surrounded by a hard shell called a chrysalis. When the chrysalis splits open, a winged adult enters the world.

egg

caterpillar

pupa

adult—black swallowtail

Like all living things, butterflies need to eat certain foods. Many adult butterflies feed on flower nectar.

EASTERN TIGER SWALLOWTAIL

Have you ever seen an eastern tiger swallowtail fluttering around a wild-flower garden or resting on an apple tree? These butterflies spend their days sipping sweet nectar. Their favorite flowers include lilacs, apple blossoms, and wild cherry blossoms. When people grow trees and other flowering plants in their yards, eastern tiger swallowtail butterflies have plenty of food.

When people have gardens in their yards, butterflies can live and grow.

Some butterflies feed on sugary tree sap.

When people work to protect forests, butterflies can live and grow.

MOURNING CLOAK

Most butterflies feed on nectar, but mourning cloaks sip tree sap and juices from rotting fruit. When wooded areas are destroyed to make room for houses and other buildings, mourning cloaks have trouble surviving. When people protect and preserve forests, mourning cloaks have a place to live and food to eat.

Many caterpillars eat only one kind of plant. Some caterpillars depend on plants that grow on burned land.

KARNER BLUE

We think of fires, tornadoes, and hurricanes as dangerous and destructive, but Karner blue caterpillars depend on these natural disasters. The caterpillars eat only wild lupine, a plant that grows best in places where other plants have been burned away or knocked over. At the Albany Pine Bush Preserve in New York, people carefully set fires to create the perfect habitat for Karner blues. Thanks to their hard work, the number of butterflies is growing.

When people let some natural wildfires burn, butterflies can live and grow.

Some caterpillars depend on plants that grow in wet places.

HESSEL'S HAIRSTREAK

Hessel's hairstreak caterpillars must eat the leaves of the Atlantic cedar, a tree that grows in swamps. In the past, people drained the water out of these wetlands. The cedar trees died, and caterpillars starved. Now that Hessel's hairstreaks are protected by law in seven states, people are preserving their wetland homes.

When people protect swamps and marshes, butterflies can live and grow.

Some caterpillars depend on plants that are poisonous to cattle and sheep.

When farmers let these plants grow in fields where their animals don't graze, butterflies can live and grow.

MONARCH

Female monarch butterflies always lay their eggs on milkweed plants. It is the only food monarch caterpillars can eat. But milkweed can give cattle and sheep a terrible stomachache. Farmers don't want sick animals, so they often kill milkweed. But if they let milkweed grow in fields where their animals aren't feeding, monarch butterflies will be able to lay their eggs on the plants.

Some caterpillars depend on plants that attack the trees people use to make paper.

THICKET HAIRSTREAK

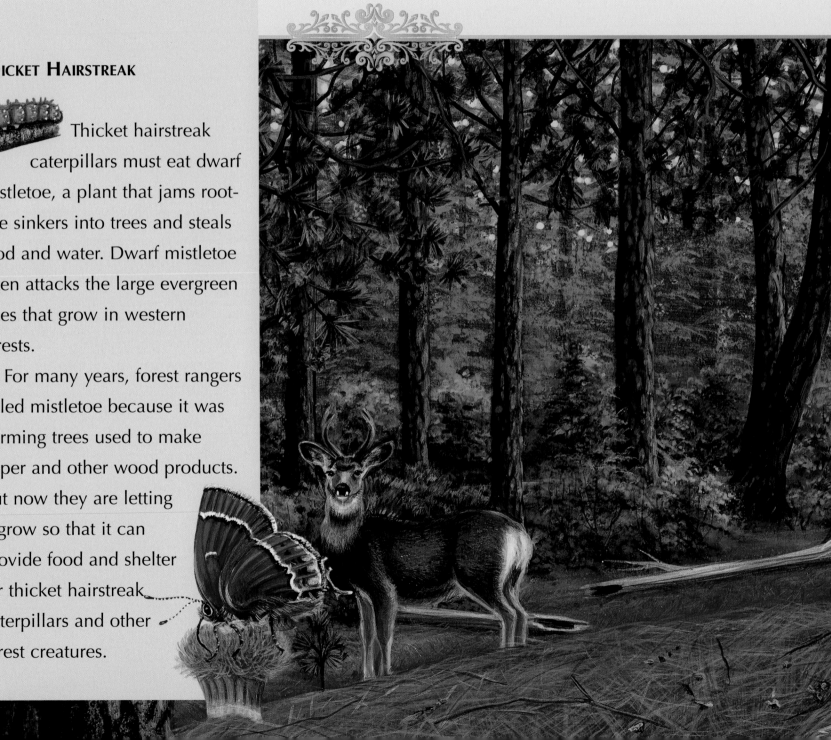

Thicket hairstreak caterpillars must eat dwarf mistletoe, a plant that jams root-like sinkers into trees and steals food and water. Dwarf mistletoe often attacks the large evergreen trees that grow in western forests.

For many years, forest rangers killed mistletoe because it was harming trees used to make paper and other wood products. But now they are letting it grow so that it can provide food and shelter for thicket hairstreak caterpillars and other forest creatures.

When people leave these plants alone, butterflies can live and grow.

Butterflies need more than just food to survive. They also need to stay safe and healthy. Some butterflies are so beautiful that people like to catch and keep them.

When laws stop people from collecting these special insects, butterflies can live and grow.

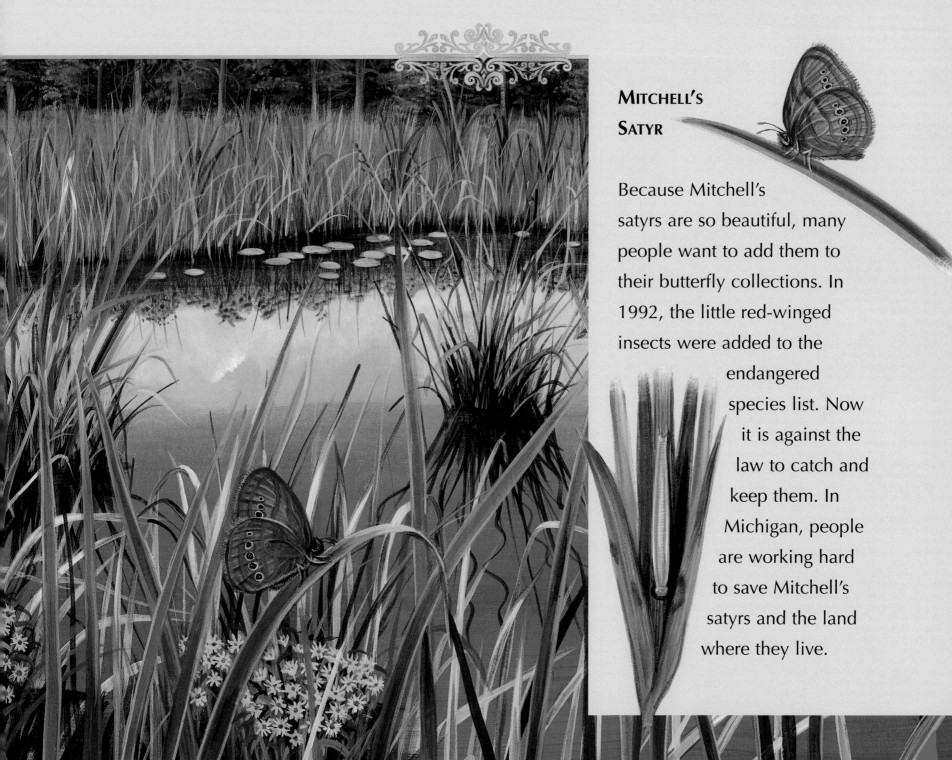

MITCHELL'S SATYR

Because Mitchell's satyrs are so beautiful, many people want to add them to their butterfly collections. In 1992, the little red-winged insects were added to the endangered species list. Now it is against the law to catch and keep them. In Michigan, people are working hard to save Mitchell's satyrs and the land where they live.

Some butterflies are harmed by chemicals used to kill other insects.

SCHAUS SWALLOWTAIL

In South Florida, giant clouds of mosquitoes fill the skies during the hot, humid summer. When workers began spraying chemicals to kill the mosquitoes, the number of Schaus swallowtails fell, too. In 1991, the spraying stopped in areas where the butterflies live. The Schaus swallowtail is still in trouble, but scientists hope it will survive.

When people stop using these chemicals or spray them very carefully,
butterflies can live and grow.

Some butterflies have trouble surviving when new plants invade the areas where they live.

When people choose native plants for their yards, butterflies can live and grow.

OREGON SILVERSPOT

Scotch broom is a plant that grows naturally in Great Britain. But because it has pretty yellow flowers and grows easily, people in the Pacific Northwest planted it in their yards. Over time, Scotch broom crowded out the plants Oregon silverspots feed on, and the butterflies had trouble surviving. Recently, zoos in Oregon and Washington began a program to replace Scotch broom with native plants, and Oregon silverspots are making a comeback.

Butterflies have trouble surviving when their natural homes are destroyed.

HARRIS'S CHECKERSPOT

Not long ago, small family farms covered much of New England. But now, people are building houses and shopping malls on the land.

In Worcester, Massachusetts, the local electric company wanted to create new places for Harris's checkerspots to live. Workers often saw butterflies flitting along the grassy paths under power lines. They asked scientists when they could mow the grass without harming butterfly eggs or caterpillars. Now butterflies can spend their whole lives in these grassy places.

Many butterflies can only live in open fields. When people create new grassy areas, butterflies can live and grow.

Some butterflies can only survive in sandy thickets near the ocean.

When people work to restore these wild places, butterflies can live and grow.

PALOS VERDES BLUE

In the 1980s, a town in California built a baseball field where the last known group of Palos Verdes blue butterflies lived. Scientists thought the little insects had disappeared forever. But in 1994, a few were spotted on a nearby Navy base. Many caring people helped plant sunflowers for the adults and deerweed for the caterpillars. Now the number of Palos Verdes blue butterflies is growing.

When too many butterflies die, other living things may also have trouble surviving.

PLANTS NEED BUTTERFLIES

As a butterfly feeds on flower nectar, it becomes dusted with pollen. When the insect flies to another flower, the pollen goes along for the ride. At the next stop, some pollen falls off the butterfly's body and lands on the flower. Then the plant can use material in the pollen to make seeds, which will grow into new plants. Butterflies and moths pollinate more plants than any other insect, except bees. Without butterflies, some flowering plants might disappear from Earth forever.

That's why it's so important to protect butterflies and the places they live.

OTHER ANIMALS NEED BUTTERFLIES

Butterflies are an important part of the food chain. Caterpillars rarely gobble up enough leaves to kill a plant. As they eat, their droppings fall to the ground and add nutrients to the soil. Both caterpillars and chrysalids are good sources of food for other insects as well as mice, opossums, skunks, birds, and toads. Adult butterflies are often eaten by spiders, dragonflies, and praying mantids.

Without butterflies, many other creatures would go hungry.

Butterflies have lived on Earth for 140 million years.

STARTING A BUTTERFLY GARDEN

If every neighbor-hood had one or two butterfly gardens, many more butterflies would have everything they need to survive. There are plenty of great books that can help you begin a butterfly garden. To get started, you'll need a water supply and a variety of plants that bloom throughout the spring, summer, and early autumn. Ask the workers at a local garden center which plants the butterflies in your area like best.

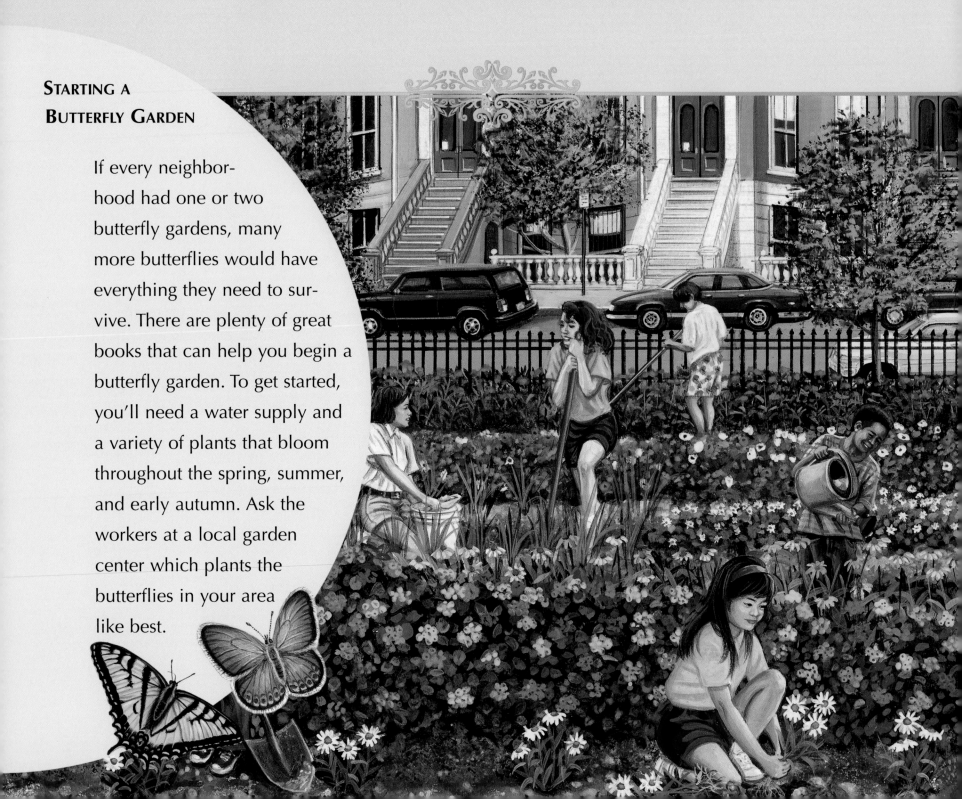

Some of the things people do can harm butterflies. But there are many ways you can help these special insects live far into the future.

HELPING BUTTERFLIES

* Do not catch and keep butterflies.
* Do not spray chemicals that could harm butterflies.
* Join a group of people that is keeping track of butterflies in your area.
* Write an article about butterflies for your school newspaper.
* Start a butterfly garden in your yard or neighborhood.

Butterfly Facts

* No one knows exactly how many kinds of butterflies live on Earth. So far, scientists have discovered more than 18,000 different species. About 750 kinds of butterflies live in North America.

* The Queen Alexandra birdwing is the world's largest butterfly. Its wings stretch wider than the pages in this book. But the tiny pygmy blue butterfly is about the size of your thumbnail.

* Most adult butterflies live less than two weeks, but monarchs and mourning cloaks can live up to 10 months.

* Some adult butterflies migrate when the days grow chilly. Other adult butterflies hibernate. Many butterflies spend the winter as eggs, caterpillars, or pupae.

* Butterflies have all kinds of tricks for protecting themselves from enemies. Can you guess why most predators stay away from the larva of eastern tiger swallowtails? Because their bodies look just like bird poop.

Selected Bibliography

Aston, Dianna Hutts. A Butterfly Is Patient. San Francisco: Chronicle Books, 2011.*

Opler, Paul. Peterson First Guide to Butterflies and Moths. Boston: Houghton Mifflin, 1998.*

Simon, Seymour. Butterflies. New York: HarperCollins, 2011.*

Sayre, April Pulley. Touch a Butterfly: Wildlife Gardening with Kids. Boston: Shambala Publications, 2013.*

Schappert, Phil. A World for Butterflies: Their Lives, Behavior, and Future. Richmond Hill, Ontario, Canada: Firefly Books, 2000.

Stewart, Melissa. How Does a Caterpillar Become a Butterfly? And Other Questions About Butterflies. New York: Sterling, 2014.*

Wright, Amy Bartlett. Peterson First Guide to Caterpillars of North America. Boston: Houghton Mifflin, 1998. *

* Recommended resources for young explorers

Websites

North American Butterfly Association: http://naba.org/

Hope for Endangered Butterfly Species: http://news.nationalgeographic.com/news/2013/13/130610-butterfly-endangered-species-insect-florida-nature-science-environment/

Acknowledgments

The author wishes to thank Brian Cassie of the North American Butterfly Association, Chris Leahy and Gail Howe of the Massachusetts Audubon Society, and David Wagner of the University of Connecticut at Storrs for their help in conceptualizing and preparing the manuscript. Thomas Emmel and Jaret Daniels of the University of Florida at Gainesville and Rudi Mattoni of the University of California in Los Angeles took time out of their busy schedules to discuss the endangered butterfly species they are studying.

The United States Geological Survey kindly provided range and habitat data for all the butterflies mentioned in this book.

The illustrator gratefully acknowledges Daniel Soyka Beran, Jaret Daniels, Michael Durham and the Oregon Zoo, Paul Opler, and Larry West, who supplied photos used as reference for many of the illustrations in this book.